THE GENDER EQUALITY SONG

by

PEZICANO

(Cover Artwork only –
no CD, no MP3 download and no
lyrics included)

You can download the cover,
reduce the size down to a CD booklet
and print it to use it as a CD cover.

Published 2014 by LULU.com

ISBN 9781326083748

THE GENDER EQUALITY SONG

by

PEZICANO

(Cover Artwork only –
no CD, no MP3 download included)

You can download the cover,
reduce the size down to a CD booklet
and print it to use it as a CD cover.

THE GENDER EQUALITY SONG

by

PEZICANO

(Cover Artwork only –
no CD, no MP3 download included)

You can download the cover,
reduce the size down to a CD booklet
and print it to use it as a CD cover.

THE GENDER EQUALITY SONG

by

PEZICANO

(Cover Artwork only –
no CD, no MP3 download included)

You can download the cover,
reduce the size down to a CD booklet
and print it to use it as a CD cover.

THE GENDER EQUALITY SONG

by

PEZICANO

(Cover Artwork only –
no CD, no MP3 download included)

You can download the cover,
reduce the size down to a CD booklet
and print it to use it as a CD cover.

THE GENDER EQUALITY SONG

by

PEZICANO

(Cover Artwork only –
no CD, no MP3 download included)

You can download the cover,
reduce the size down to a CD booklet
and print it to use it as a CD cover.

THE GENDER EQUALITY SONG

by

PEZICANO

(Cover Artwork only –
no CD, no MP3 download included)

You can download the cover,
reduce the size down to a CD booklet
and print it to use it as a CD cover.

THE GENDER EQUALITY SONG

by

PEZICANO

(Cover Artwork only –
no CD, no MP3 download included)

You can download the cover,
reduce the size down to a CD booklet
and print it to use it as a CD cover.

THE GENDER EQUALITY SONG

by

PEZICANO

(Cover Artwork only –
no CD, no MP3 download included)

You can download the cover,
reduce the size down to a CD booklet
and print it to use it as a CD cover.

THE GENDER EQUALITY SONG

by

PEZICANO

(Cover Artwork only –
no CD, no MP3 download included)

You can download the cover,
reduce the size down to a CD booklet
and print it to use it as a CD cover.

THE GENDER EQUALITY SONG

by

PEZICANO

(Cover Artwork only –
no CD, no MP3 download included)

You can download the cover,
reduce the size down to a CD booklet
and print it to use it as a CD cover.

THE GENDER EQUALITY SONG

by

PEZICANO

(Cover Artwork only –
no CD, no MP3 download included)

You can download the cover,
reduce the size down to a CD booklet
and print it to use it as a CD cover.

THE GENDER EQUALITY SONG

by

PEZICANO

(Cover Artwork only –
no CD, no MP3 download included)

You can download the cover,
reduce the size down to a CD booklet
and print it to use it as a CD cover.

THE GENDER EQUALITY SONG

by

PEZICANO

(Cover Artwork only –
no CD, no MP3 download included)

You can download the cover,
reduce the size down to a CD booklet
and print it to use it as a CD cover.

THE GENDER EQUALITY SONG

by

PEZICANO

(Cover Artwork only –
no CD, no MP3 download included)

You can download the cover,
reduce the size down to a CD booklet
and print it to use it as a CD cover.

THE GENDER EQUALITY SONG

by

PEZICANO

(Cover Artwork only –
no CD, no MP3 download included)

You can download the cover,
reduce the size down to a CD booklet
and print it to use it as a CD cover.

THE GENDER EQUALITY SONG

by

PEZICANO

(Cover Artwork only –
no CD, no MP3 download included)

You can download the cover,
reduce the size down to a CD booklet
and print it to use it as a CD cover.

THE GENDER EQUALITY SONG

by

PEZICANO

(Cover Artwork only –
no CD, no MP3 download included)

You can download the cover,
reduce the size down to a CD booklet
and print it to use it as a CD cover.

THE GENDER EQUALITY SONG

by

PEZICANO

(Cover Artwork only –
no CD, no MP3 download included)

You can download the cover,
reduce the size down to a CD booklet
and print it to use it as a CD cover.

THE GENDER EQUALITY SONG

by

PEZICANO

(Cover Artwork only –
no CD, no MP3 download included)

You can download the cover,
reduce the size down to a CD booklet
and print it to use it as a CD cover.

THE GENDER EQUALITY SONG

by

PEZICANO

(Cover Artwork only –
no CD, no MP3 download included)

You can download the cover,
reduce the size down to a CD booklet
and print it to use it as a CD cover.

THE GENDER EQUALITY SONG

by

PEZICANO

(Cover Artwork only –
no CD, no MP3 download included)

You can download the cover,
reduce the size down to a CD booklet
and print it to use it as a CD cover.

THE GENDER EQUALITY SONG

by

PEZICANO

(Cover Artwork only –
no CD, no MP3 download included)

You can download the cover,
reduce the size down to a CD booklet
and print it to use it as a CD cover.

THE GENDER EQUALITY SONG

by

PEZICANO

(Cover Artwork only –
no CD, no MP3 download included)

You can download the cover,
reduce the size down to a CD booklet
and print it to use it as a CD cover.

THE GENDER EQUALITY SONG

by

PEZICANO

(Cover Artwork only –
no CD, no MP3 download included)

You can download the cover,
reduce the size down to a CD booklet
and print it to use it as a CD cover.

THE GENDER EQUALITY SONG

by

PEZICANO

(Cover Artwork only –
no CD, no MP3 download included)

You can download the cover,
reduce the size down to a CD booklet
and print it to use it as a CD cover.

THE GENDER EQUALITY SONG

by

PEZICANO

(Cover Artwork only –
no CD, no MP3 download included)

You can download the cover,
reduce the size down to a CD booklet
and print it to use it as a CD cover.

THE GENDER EQUALITY SONG

by

PEZICANO

(Cover Artwork only –
no CD, no MP3 download included)

You can download the cover,
reduce the size down to a CD booklet
and print it to use it as a CD cover.

THE GENDER EQUALITY SONG

by

PEZICANO

(Cover Artwork only –
no CD, no MP3 download included)

You can download the cover,
reduce the size down to a CD booklet
and print it to use it as a CD cover.